D1710405

TEEN MENTAL HEALTH™

drug abuse

Bruce Edelfield and
Tracey J. Moosa

ROSEN
PUBLISHING®

New York

Published in 2012 by The Rosen Publishing Group, Inc.
29 East 21st Street, New York, NY 10010

Library of Congress Cataloging-in-Publication Data

Edelfield, Bruce.
Drug abuse / Bruce Edelfield, Tracey J. Moosa.—1st ed.
      p. cm.—(Teen mental health)
Includes bibliographical references and index.
ISBN 978-1-4488-4590-3 (library binding)
1. Teenagers—Drug use—Juvenile literature. 2. Drug abuse—
Prevention—Juvenile literature. I. Moosa, Tracey J. II. Title.
HV5824.Y68E315 2011
362.290835—dc22

                                                                2011000540

Manufactured in the United States of America

CPSIA Compliance Information: Batch #S11YA: For further information, contact Rosen Publishing, New York, New York,
at 1-800-237-9932.

Drug Abuse

contents

chapter one

Drugs and Their Dangers

Drugs are substances you take—whether manufactured or from a natural source—that change the way you think, feel, or act. For legal drugs, some substances require a prescription; others can be bought by anyone over-the-counter. A few drugs are legal but have certain limitations. In the United States, for example, there are minimum ages for the legal use of both alcohol and tobacco products.

All drugs can be harmful: legal drugs that are taken for too long or in too large a dosage, medicines used without a prescription, or illegal drugs used to get high. Any drug, legal or not, can be abused. Drug abuse can cause a host of physical and psychological problems. Below is a discussion of the types of drugs and the short-term and long-term effects that they can have on the body and mind.

The Depressing Side of Alcohol

Alcohol (ethanol) is a drug teens abuse often. Since alcohol often causes a loss of inhibition—that is, it makes you act more spontaneous and less shy—you may think of it as a stimulant. But alcohol is actually a depressant. It slows down the heart rate as well as the central nervous system. Alcohol is absorbed into the bloodstream and is carried throughout the body. It impairs coordination and memory and dulls the senses. Drinking too much alcohol affects your speech and balance. It also results in impaired judgment, which can lead to car accidents, drownings, falls, suicides, and homicides. Pregnant women who abuse alcohol may cause serious birth defects in their babies.

Millions of people, among them many teens, abuse alcohol. Alcohol is usually the first drug that teens try, and many are unaware of its harmful effects. Some people mistakenly believe there is a difference between "hard" alcohol, such as whisky, vodka, rum, and gin, and "soft" alcohol, such as beer, cider, and wine. But a glass of wine or beer contains the same amount of alcohol as a shot of vodka, and the alcohol affects you the same way.

Certain alcoholic drinks are very sweet and deceptive. You may not feel that there is a lot of alcohol in a drink if it doesn't have a strong flavor. This may lead to

Alcohol is a depressant, and once the "buzz" wears off, a physical and emotional crash follows. Overconsumption of alcohol can lead to deadly accidents, dangerous behavior, blackouts, and even fatal poisoning.

consuming more drinks than you planned. Drinking caffeinated alcoholic drinks can also result in the overconsumption of alcohol. This is because the stimulant effect of the caffeine keeps people awake and drinking past the point beyond which they'd ordinarily go home, fall asleep, or pass out. Binge drinking (consuming a lot of alcohol in a short period) is especially dangerous. It can cause alcohol poisoning, coma, and even death. Binge drinking occurs frequently among teens.

Marijuana: Paranoia, Memory Loss, Cancer, and Respiratory Disease

Marijuana, commonly known as weed, pot, and grass, is the most popular illicit drug among teens. Tetrahydrocannabinol (THC), the main active ingredient in marijuana, increases heart rate and

Getting high comes at an enormous cost. Marijuana use can lead to lung and oral cancers, long-lasting cognitive impairment, and chronic memory loss.

distorts your sense of your surroundings. It also causes memory loss and can make you feel paranoid, or irrationally suspicious of others. Over time, marijuana abuse damages your respiratory system, causing breathing problems and possibly lung or mouth cancer. It can also suppress the immune system, which protects your body from disease and illness. In addition, for many teens, marijuana seems to act as a "gateway drug," meaning that its use opens the door to the possibility of trying more dangerous illicit substances like cocaine or heroin.

Methamphetamine: A Toxic Cocktail

Methamphetamine is a powerful and highly addictive synthetic drug. In its crystal form (also known as "ice" or "glass"), methamphetamine is one of the most widely abused drugs in the United States, especially on the West

Coast and in the rural Midwest. Crystal meth is made of volatile, toxic chemicals, which are mixed in differing combinations. Since the chemicals are relatively easy to get, and the recipe is not too hard to follow, illegal "meth labs" are increasingly common all over the country.

Crystal meth is most often smoked in a pipe, but it is also injected and snorted. Smoking results in an almost instantaneous delivery of the drug to the brain. It gives users a feeling of exhilaration and makes them feel sharp and highly focused. The euphoric feelings may last from two to sixteen hours. Overdosing, however, can lead to heart palpitations and severe convulsions, followed by circulatory and respiratory collapse, coma, and even death.

Under the influence of methamphetamine, users often become obsessive or suffer from extreme paranoia. They also undergo mood swings and short-term memory loss. In addition, many crystal meth users report having unprotected sex, often with an unfamiliar partner. This activity greatly increases the risk of contracting sexually transmitted diseases, including HIV, the virus that causes AIDS. Recent reports claim that crystal meth has been a factor in almost half of the new AIDS cases in the United States.

If you have seen pictures of the progression of a person on crystal meth, you know the physical toll the drug takes on a person's body, both inside and out. Crystal meth abuse can cause you to lose all your money, your reputation, your health, and even your teeth. A condition called "meth mouth" occurs when the drug dries out the user's saliva, leading to rapid tooth decay. Jaw grinding, smoking, and the poor hygiene and diet of typical users also accelerate tooth decay.

Hallucinogens: Bad Trips

Hallucinogens are a class of commonly abused illegal drugs. These include LSD (acid), PCP (angel dust), marijuana, mushrooms, mescaline, and the so-called "club drugs" ecstasy and ketamine. When you take a hallucinogen, your sense of time and place becomes distorted, and you see, hear, and feel things that aren't really there. Hallucinogens increase heart rate and blood pressure. They impair muscle coordination and pain awareness, and they may cause severe anxiety and insomnia.

People high on hallucinogens often put themselves and others in danger by taking unreasonable risks or by acting violently or in unexpected ways. The effects of hallucinogens are very unpredictable and can last up to twelve hours. Some hallucinogens, including LSD and PCP, may lead to flashbacks, which cause you to slip back into a drug "trip," even though you may not have done the drug for weeks, months, years, or even decades.

Club Drugs: When the Party's Over

Club drugs are common at dance clubs and other party scenes because they keep users awake and energized throughout the night. The most common club drugs come in pill or liquid form, which makes them easier to abuse than drugs that are smoked or injected.

The hallucinogens ecstasy (MDMA) and Special K (ketamine hydrochloride) are two club drugs that have become popular among some teens. Ecstasy is a powerful stimulant and mood changer that speeds up the body's

9

regulatory systems and alters the user's perception. It may make the user feel both uplifted and relaxed, but the effects of ecstasy vary considerably from one person to the next. The happy feelings of the first few hours diminish as the drug wears off, and users typically end up feeling dejected, worn out, and sometimes extremely depressed. Ecstasy pills sold on the street are often "dirty," meaning they may also contain heroin, cocaine, speed, or other drugs.

Ecstasy users may dance for hours without ever replenishing body fluids, so dehydration is a serious problem. The dehydration contributes to the tremendous strain the drug already puts on the heart, liver, and kidneys. Several ecstasy users have died of dehydration when on ecstasy.

Special K is an anesthetic (a substance used to numb the body) used legally by veterinarians and doctors during surgery. Special K usually comes in liquid or powder form, which can be snorted or dissolved in a drink.

Like ecstasy, Special K distorts the senses and causes intense hallucinations. It also causes impaired judgment and coordination, which may lead to serious accidents. Since Special K and ecstasy prevent users from feeling pain, people high on these drugs can hurt themselves without even knowing it.

In addition to ecstasy and Special K, two other drugs, GHB (gammahydroxybutyrate) and Rohypnol (roofies), have become popular as club drugs. GHB was originally used by bodybuilders as an anabolic (muscle-building) steroid. However, it became popular as a recreational drug as more people abused it for its relaxing effects. A small dose may make a user feel peaceful and uninhibited.

However, larger doses may lead to disorientation, nausea, muscle spasms, numbness, and vomiting. Other side effects include hallucinations, vertigo (dizziness and loss of balance), skin rashes, and stomach problems. GHB lowers blood pressure and may make breathing difficult for some users. Overdosing can lead to a loss of consciousness and coma. For someone who has asthma or any

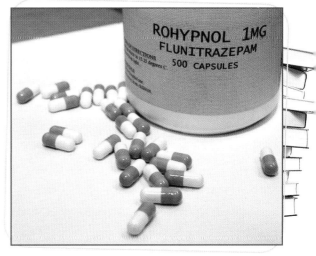

Originally developed as an anti-insomnia drug, Rohypnol has more recently been abused in conjunction with alcohol to create a powerful and very dangerous sedative effect.

respiratory or low blood pressure disorder, taking this drug can be extremely dangerous and possibly fatal.

Rohypnol is a prescription sedative that is illegal in the United States. It is legally prescribed in Europe and Latin America for the treatment of severe sleeping disorders. Rohypnol is a benzodiazepine, a class of drugs that suppress the central nervous and respiratory systems, slowing down breathing and heart rates. Used on its own, Rohypnol is unlikely to be fatal. However, when combined with other drugs, such as alcohol or marijuana, the physical risks increase greatly. Rohypnol is often slipped into the drinks of unsuspecting women, who then pass out and are taken advantage of. This is why it is often referred to as the "date rape drug."

11

Sedative-Hypnotics: Abusing Prescription Depressants

Sedative-hypnotics (sleeping pills) and anti-anxiety medications include barbiturates and benzodiazepines, such as Rohypnol. Benzodiazepines are prescribed for muscle strain, tension, sleep problems, and anxiety or panic attacks. In addition to Rohypnol and Valium, other common trade names are Ativan, Halcion, Klonopin, Librium, Restoril, and Xanax. When used correctly and under a doctor's care and supervision, these depressants safely help many people.

Sedative-hypnotics depress the central nervous system. Their effects are similar to those of alcohol. Users feel euphoric (very happy) at first, but then they become sleepy. They may slur their speech and have difficulty focusing their eyes. Both legal and illegal depressants can pose great risks when used improperly. Depressants often lead to dependence and addiction, and sudden withdrawal from depressants can cause seizures and death.

Abuse of sedative-hypnotics may cause many of the symptoms of alcohol abuse, including depression, insomnia, moodiness, and apathy. Combining sedative-hypnotics with alcohol is especially dangerous because it leads to an effect called potentiation. This means the effect of the two depressants taken together is stronger than the combined effect of each taken separately. For someone who has low tolerance to depressants, the potentiation effect can cause liver damage. In severe cases, potentiation may lead to a blackout, a coma, or death.

Inhalants: Ingesting Deadly Toxins

Inhalants are substances that are sniffed. Most of these chemicals are not meant to be used to produce psycho-active (mind-altering) effects. Inhalants include model airplane glue, nail polish remover, gasoline, plastic cement, lighter fluid, spray paint, Freon, and nitrous oxide. Many cleaning products are also abused as inhalants.

These chemicals are easy to buy and use, but even a one-time use can be fatal. Inhalants increase heart rate, making the user feel dizzy and lightheaded. They can also lead to asphyxia, or a stoppage in the flow of oxygen to the brain. This can cause a user to become unconscious. Other consequences of inhalant use include nausea, lack of coor-dination, and decreased heart rate. Deep inhaling or heavy use (called "huffing") may cause abnormal thinking and can lead to violent behavior. In addition to causing breathing problems, highly concentrated inhalants can cause heart attacks and suffocation. Over time a user's brain, lungs, liver, and kidneys may also suffer serious damage.

Narcotics: Painful Addiction to Painkillers

Narcotics, which include heroin, opium, methadone, and morphine, are painkillers. Like depressants, narcotics slow down the central nervous system. They are among the most addictive drugs because they are very potent and cause the body to have strong cravings. Narcotics are usually smoked or injected, leading to an immediate rush. At first, users feel euphoric and drowsy, but dangerous side effects may follow, including breathing problems, convulsions, coma, and even death.

Heroin is particularly dangerous. The quality of street heroin varies, so an amount that gets the user high one day could be the same amount that kills him or her the next. In addition, heroin abusers face other risks because they usually take the drug by injection. If the needle is not disinfected between uses, an infected user can pass deadly diseases like HIV or hepatitis C to another user.

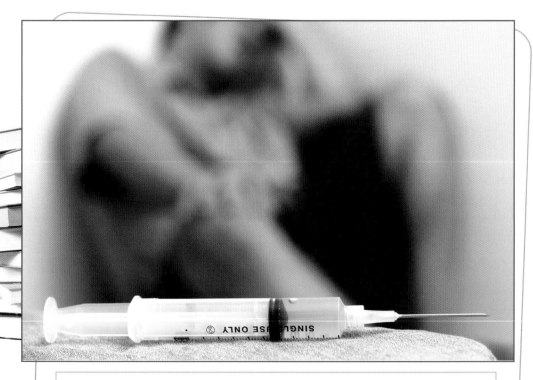

Heroin is dangerous and deadly enough in its own right, but the dangers increase dramatically when users share needles. The result can be the transmission of disease, including tetanus, hepatitis, and HIV/AIDS.

Quitting narcotics leads to withdrawal symptoms, which are usually severe. These include tremors, cramps, muscle spasms, nervous movements, chills, and sweating. Some who have trouble quitting heroin may try methadone therapy. Methadone is a synthetic opiate that fulfills the craving for heroin while allowing the user to avoid the withdrawal symptoms that come when one quits completely (called quitting "cold turkey"). Methadone users have to report to a methadone clinic, daily in most cases, to take the drug in front of a nurse. Methadone comes in either a biscuit or syrup form, which is usually mixed with juice and swallowed.

There are other, newer prescription medications that are similar to methadone but are used under a doctor's supervision, rather than at a clinic. Two of the more promising drugs are buprenorphine (brand name: Buprenex). The Buprenex contains naloxone, a substance that immediately causes withdrawal symptoms if another narcotic is taken with it.

Nicotine: A Cancer-Causing Stimulant

Nicotine is found in cigarettes, cigars, snuff, and chewing tobacco. Since 1998, it has been illegal for anyone under the age of eighteen to buy these and other tobacco products in the United States. Some people smoke cigarettes to reduce tension, but nicotine actually has the opposite effect, increasing heart rate and blood pressure.

Smoking increases the risks of heart disease; emphysema; stroke; and cancer of the mouth, throat, lungs, uterus, and bladder. The nicotine in cigarettes is extremely addictive, and cigarette smoke contains hundreds of harmful chemicals, including gases that stick to the insides of the lungs.

Steroids: Building Muscle, Destroying Health

Steroids are naturally occurring substances produced by the adrenal and sex glands. They can also be manufactured synthetically. Some diseases, such as anemia, are treated safely and successfully using manufactured steroids. However, one class of steroids—anabolic steroids—promote muscle growth, making bodies bigger, stronger, and faster. For this reason, athletes abuse anabolic steroids to heighten performance. Steroid abuse can cause many health problems, including liver tumors, high blood pressure, and severe acne. In addition, steroid abusers often experience periods of extreme paranoia, anger (called "'roid rage"), and hallucinations. Long-term use can cause liver disease, cancer, and heart attacks.

Stimulants: Speed Kills

Stimulants include street drugs like cocaine, crack, and amphetamines (including methamphetamine), as well as prescription drugs such as Benzedrine and Dexedrine. Cocaine can be snorted, injected, or smoked. Crack, too, is smoked. Amphetamines can be snorted, injected, smoked, or swallowed. Ritalin, which is prescribed for attention deficit disorder (ADD) and attention deficit/hyperactivity disorder (ADHD), is an amphetamine. If you have either of these disorders, the amphetamine

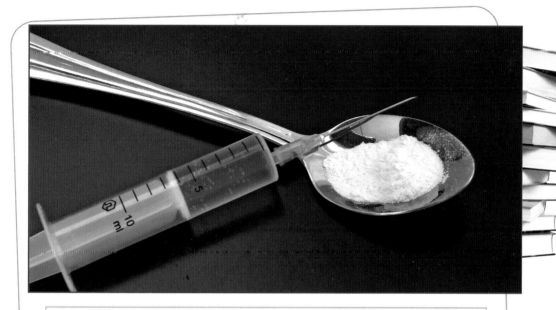

Cocaine is typically found in powdered form and snorted, though it can also be injected and smoked. There is no safe way to ingest cocaine. It can lead to fatal overdoses, long-term disease, and ruinous life decisions.

adjusts chemical levels in your brain, allowing you to concentrate better and think more clearly. However, if you do not have ADD or ADHD, taking Ritalin or any of the other common ADD/ADHD medications is drug abuse.

Stimulants increase blood pressure and heart rate, making you feel euphoric and alert at first. This explains why amphetamines are often called pep pills. Later, however, you may become anxious, depressed, or violent. You may also suffer from hallucinations or convulsions. After a while, regular users often lose interest in food and sex. Other dangerous effects include heart attacks, strokes, and respiratory failure.

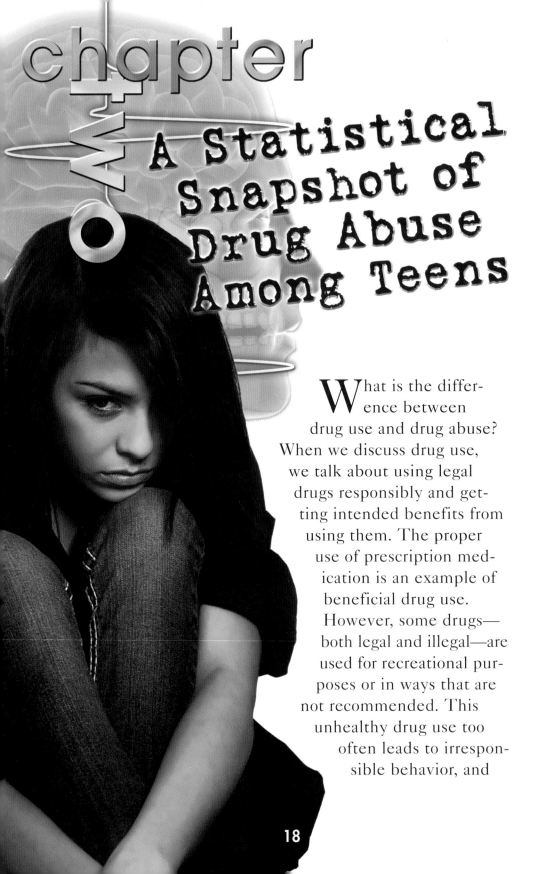

chapter two

A Statistical Snapshot of Drug Abuse Among Teens

What is the difference between drug use and drug abuse? When we discuss drug use, we talk about using legal drugs responsibly and getting intended benefits from using them. The proper use of prescription medication is an example of beneficial drug use. However, some drugs—both legal and illegal—are used for recreational purposes or in ways that are not recommended. This unhealthy drug use too often leads to irresponsible behavior, and when drug use leads to irresponsible behavior, it is considered drug abuse.

It is widely known that drug abuse among teens is a major problem in the United States. The National Institute on Drug Abuse (NIDA) prepares *Monitoring the Future* (MTF), an annual report that compares information on teen drug abuse from one year to the next. According to the 2010 MTF report, the proportion of teens using illicit (illegal) drugs is on the rise. About 16 percent of students in the eighth grade, 30 percent in the tenth grade, and 38 percent in the twelfth grade reported using an illicit drug in the past twelve months. These figures all represent increases over the previous three years. Twenty-one percent of eighth graders, 37 percent of tenth graders, and 48 percent of twelfth graders reporting having used illegal drugs at least once in their lives. Almost half of all high school seniors admitted to using drugs at least once, and about a third had done so in the last twelve months.

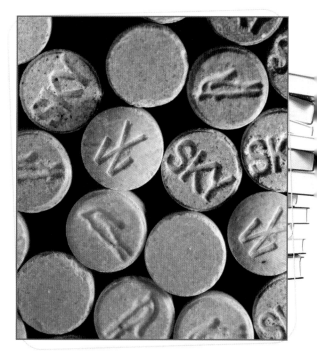

Though billed as a club drug, ecstasy has a way of killing the party, literally. In high doses, it can lead to liver, kidney, or cardiovascular system failure, or death.

The 2010 *Monitoring the Future* survey results revealed a disturbing upward trend in teen drug use, reversing promising declines earlier in the decade. Much of the increase is due to rising marijuana use and the renewed popularity of ecstasy. Use of ecstasy had been in decline for several years from its peak in 2001, due largely to widely publicized health and safety concerns and high-profile overdose deaths. Now, however, there is a general—and highly erroneous—feeling among teens that both marijuana and ecstasy are safe, so usage is again increasing. Another disturbing trend is the increase in heroin use among twelfth graders.

Good News and Bad News

Not all the news in the 2010 *Monitoring the Future* report is bad, however. Teen drinking rates—especially the incidence of binge drinking—continue to decline and are now at a historic low point. Consumption of once popular flavored alcohol drinks has waned. However, caffeinated alcoholic beverages that result in heavier-than-normal drinking due to increased wakefulness have become a major concern, and the U.S. Food and Drug Administration (FDA) is trying to crack down on manufacturers. Use of many kinds of illicit drugs—like cocaine—and the misuse of prescription drugs—like sedatives and the amphetamines Ritalin and Adderall—are also waning.

Yet demonstrating how difficult it is to build upon promising gains like this, the use of other kinds of illicit and prescription drugs is holding steady. Usage rates for

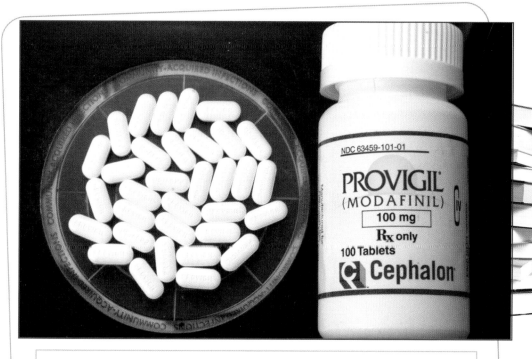

Though prescribed for the sleep disorder narcolepsy, Provigil is increasingly being abused by teens as a stimulant.

drugs like the highly addictive painkillers Vicodin and OxyContin, inhalants, LSD and other hallucinogens, PCP, crack, methamphetamine and crystal meth, "club drugs" (like Rohypnol, GHB, and ketamine), steroids, and over-the-counter cough and cold medicines have remained essentially unchanged. In addition, the use of two new drugs seems to be increasing among teens: the herbal hallucinogenic Salvia (which teen star Miley Cyrus was filmed using in 2010) and the prescription stimulant Provigil.

Just the Facts

Some other findings in the 2010 *Monitoring the Future* survey include:

- Seven percent of eighth graders, 12 percent of tenth graders, and 17 percent of twelfth graders used an illicit drug other than marijuana in the previous year. Eleven percent of eighth graders, 17 percent of tenth graders, and 25 percent of twelfth graders have used an illicit drug other than marijuana at least once in their lives.
- Daily, monthly, yearly, and lifetime marijuana use rose for all three grades.
- One percent of eighth graders, 3 percent of tenth graders, and 6 percent of twelfth graders used marijuana on a daily basis. One out of sixteen high school seniors used marijuana every day.
- In the previous year, 1.6 percent of eighth graders, 2.2 percent of tenth graders, and 2.9 percent of twelfth graders used cocaine. This is far less than usage rates in the 1980s and 1990s.
- In the previous year, 4.8 percent of high school seniors used barbiturates (sedatives) and 5.6 percent used tranquilizers.
- In the previous year, 2.7 percent of eighth graders, 7.7 percent of tenth graders, and 8 percent of twelfth graders used Vicodin. The corresponding rates for use of OxyContin in the previous year by grade were 2.1 percent, 4.6 percent, and 5.1 percent.

- LSD was taken by 2.6 percent of high school seniors in the previous year.
- Cough and cold medicines were misused/abused by 3.2 percent of eighth graders, 5.1 percent of tenth graders, and 6.6 percent of twelfth graders in the previous year.
- Salvia was used by 1.7 percent of eighth graders, 3.7 percent of tenth graders, and 5.5 percent of twelfth graders in the previous year. In 2010, 1.3 percent of high school seniors misused/abused Provigil.
- In the previous year, 0.5 percent of eighth graders, 1 percent of tenth graders, and 1.5 percent of twelfth graders took steroids. The corresponding numbers for boys only by grade were 0.7 percent, 1.3 percent, and 2.5 percent.

chapter three

What Spurs Drug Abuse

When something is forbidden, you may want to try it even more, especially if your parents are the ones saying, "Don't do that." Everyone rebels against an authority figure at some point. It's one way to find out who you are and create your own identity. Using drugs can be an especially tempting way to rebel because they promise to make you feel good.

You might believe that you are "expanding your horizons" or "increasing your creativity" by experimenting with drugs.

But most teens don't think about the harmful effects drug use can have on all areas of the body. Trying drugs just to see what they feel like is very dangerous and can lead to serious, long-term problems.

Trying to Fit In

The most common reason that teens start using and continue to use drugs is peer pressure, or influence from friends. You may find that a lot of what your friends do has an effect on you. If you hang out with people who use drugs, it can be

While drinking might seem like fun at first, it often ends in sickness, depression, and physical and emotional pain.

pretty hard not to use drugs and still feel accepted by people in that group. Wanting to fit in or look cool to others, you start using drugs. Sometimes it feels easier to give in than to take a stand.

It's hard to deal with peer pressure because it can be very subtle. In other words, many teens may not realize or recognize when they're giving in to peer pressure. You may tell yourself you will try marijuana or alcohol just this one time to get people off your back. But soon these

Lindsay Lohan leaves court following a probation hearing related to her chronic substance abuse problems.

activities become a regular occurrence, and then you don't feel comfortable not using when you're with your friends. Your friends may make you feel unwelcome if you don't participate in their drug use.

Emulating Celebrities

You've probably heard or read about movie stars, musicians, models, and athletes who use drugs. Television, radio, magazines, and newspapers are filled with their stories, which may have a strong influence on your view of drugs. Such popular movies as *Pineapple Express*, *Harold & Kumar Go to White Castle*, and *Get Him to the Greek* show drug use as a normal part of life. As far back as the 1920s, popular musicians were known to use marijuana, and drug use in the music scene has only increased since then. Sometimes being caught using drugs gives people more publicity and even a kind of "street credibility" than they had before. Miley Cyrus and Lindsay Lohan are examples of this phenomenon. Seeing all these "cool" and famous people abusing drugs may lead you to underestimate the danger that these drugs pose and emulate them by mimicking their actions. This is how some teens start taking drugs.

Two drugs that teens often try first are nicotine (cigarettes) and alcohol. Because these drugs are legal for adults, many teens may not understand their harmful effects. Worse, some studies show that once a person tries one drug, he or she is usually willing to try other, more harmful drugs. They call the initial drugs, like nicotine or alcohol, gateway drugs because they provide an opening for the use of harder, more dangerous drugs.

Self-Medicating

Being a teen isn't always easy. You may feel that your parents don't understand you, or that school is boring and a waste of time. You may be feeling depressed or anxious about a problem with your friends, your family, a boyfriend or girlfriend, a bully, or even your health. When things go wrong, you may look for easy solutions or a way to escape. You may turn to drugs to get some immediate relief from your depression or anxiety. This is a very dangerous step to take. If you try a drug and it eases your pain or relieves your unhappiness for a few hours, you may start using drugs regularly in an effort to cope with your situation. But drugs are not solutions: when the drugs wear off, the problems remain and even deepen and intensify. In the end, drug use will only make your problems worse.

Copying Parental Behavior

Some teens grow up in homes where they often see their parents drink alcohol or use other drugs. Some parents may use alcohol responsibly, as many people do. But many others have problems with alcohol or drugs. Teens with substance-abusing parents may believe that drugs and alcohol are acceptable ways to cope with problems. They have learned this behavior from their parents.

Studies show that the biological children of substance abusers are at higher risk of drug abuse and addiction than children whose parents don't have problems with drugs or alcohol. Children of abusers who develop their own substance abuse problems do so at an earlier age, and their problems tend to be more severe. This indicates that a tendency to abuse substances may be genetically inherited. However, while these children are at higher risk for alcohol or drug-abuse problems, genetic factors alone are not to blame. Scientists believe that the causes of abuse and addiction involve a combination of several factors, both genetic and environmental.

Regardless of why you began abusing drugs, now is the time to get help. Speak with a counselor or therapist about the best places to seek professional help in kicking the habit. Also check out the resources in the "For More Information" section of this book to find out where to go to get the help you need.

chapter four

Drug Abuse and the Effects on the Body, Mind, and Emotions

Drug abuse causes problems in all aspects of your life. It affects your physical health and well-being, your mental and emotional health, and your relationships with loved ones. Physically, the dangers of drug abuse can have both immediate and long-term effects.

Short-Term Dangers

Depending on the substance ingested,

the immediate dangers of drug abuse include dehydration, asphyxiation (suffocation), lung damage, seizures, comas, and heart failure. In addition, some drugs affect physical coordination, or the ability to control your movements. For example, alcohol, marijuana, depressants, narcotics, and inhalants can slow your reaction time and weaken your control over your muscles. It is not safe to drive a car, operate machinery, or be involved in any other activity that requires good coordination when under the influence of drugs or alcohol. If you are high on these drugs, you increase the chances of having accidents affecting yourself and others.

Long-Term Dangers

In the long term, drugs suppress (lower) your immune system, the body's main protection against illness and disease. Drug abusers are more likely to develop respiratory illnesses like pneumonia. In addition, drug abuse may cause internal damage that will affect you for the rest of your life.

For example, alcohol abuse permanently damages the tissues of your heart, liver, and brain. Caffeine can raise your blood pressure, make you jittery, and cause headaches. Cigarettes cause ulcers, bronchitis, emphysema, heart disease, and many forms of cancer. Marijuana smoke damages the lungs and may contribute to heart disease. Methamphetamine abuse causes skin rashes and high blood pressure as well as gastrointestinal problems like diarrhea and nausea, which may persist even after you quit using the drug. Hallucinogens can cause heart and lung failure and convulsions. Inhalants—such as glue or

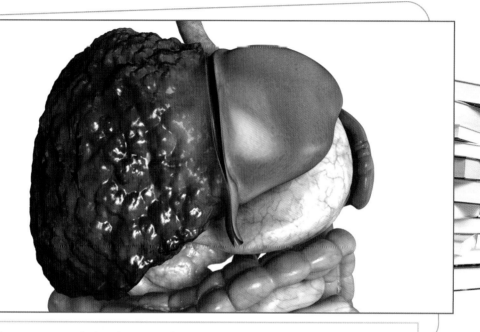

This image of the human liver reveals cirrhosis—an often fatal scarring of the liver caused by alcohol abuse.

gasoline—do serious damage to the cells in your brain, lungs, liver, and kidneys. Steroids cause liver tumors, cysts, and heart disease. Painkillers can cause irregular heartbeat and respiratory failure. Abusing stimulants can cause blood clots in the brain, which can lead to strokes. How many more reasons do you need to avoid drug abuse?

Increased Possibility of Contracting HIV and Developing AIDS

You cannot contract the human immunodeficiency virus (HIV) that causes acquired immunodeficiency syndrome (AIDS) from drugs themselves. However, if you inject

When substance abuse takes over your life, your body, and your emotions, it's time to get immediate professional help.

drugs—such as heroin—with a hypodermic needle, you are putting yourself at a very high risk of contracting HIV. Needles are often shared among users and are not properly cleaned between uses, so the virus is easily transmitted from one person to another through microscopic amounts of blood left on the needle.

HIV and AIDS have spread at a rapid rate nationally and worldwide. The most recent available statistics from the Centers for Disease Control and Prevention indicate that more than one-third—34 percent—of all new HIV infections in the United States occurred among people between the ages of 13 and 29. Since the AIDS crisis began, intravenous drug use has accounted for 36 percent of all AIDS cases. The most recent statistics indicate that IV drug use continues to be a leading cause of AIDS, attributed to 28 percent of all new AIDS cases. There is no cure for AIDS.

The Psychological and Emotional Effects of Drug Abuse

Drugs affect how you think and feel. Drug abuse causes several types of mental and emotional problems, including memory problems, guilt and depression, anxiety, and denial. In addition, drug abuse can cause you to be apathetic. This means you lose interest in school, sports, favorite activities, friends and family, and social life. Abusers often lose interest in everything—except drugs. Many drop out of school or lose their jobs. You may know someone who went to school with you, got into drugs, and then dropped out.

MYTHS AND FACTS

Myth: You have to use drugs for a long time before they can really hurt you.

Fact: You can overdose the first time you use a drug. You can have a heart attack, seizure, or stroke the first time you use a drug. You can be infected by HIV, the virus that causes AIDS, the first time you use a needle to inject a drug.

Myth: Drugs relieve stress. They help deal with problems.

Fact: Drugs only make people temporarily forget about their troubles. When the high is gone, the problem is still there and has perhaps become worse. In fact, many additional and often more serious problems develop, thanks to drug abuse.

Myth: As soon as a person feels normal again, all of the drug is out of the body.

Fact: Long after the effects of the drug stop being felt, the drug can still be present in the body. Heroin and cocaine can still be in your blood for three days to a week after using them, depending on how much you did. Benzodiazepines can be in your system for up to a month. You can test positive for marijuana up to three months after the last time you smoked or otherwise ingested it.

chapter five

When Abuse Becomes Addiction

Many drugs lower inhibitions, the internal warning signals that establish self-control, personal safety, and socially appropriate behavior. If those inhibitions are taken away, you may be more likely to try other drugs, engage in criminal behavior, or have unprotected sex. Drugs affect your ability to weigh the consequences of your actions. You may find yourself dealing with a jail sentence, an unwanted pregnancy, a sexually transmitted disease, or worse. If you're abusing drugs, it can happen without your realizing it. The longer you use drugs, the more you need them. Soon drugs take control of your life, and you find you can't stop using. At this point, you need to seek immediate professional help. Go to a rehabilitation clinic, join a support group, meet with drug and alcohol abuse therapists.

Physical and Psychological Addiction

Drug addiction can be either psychological or physical. Both types of addiction make it very difficult to stop using. Psychological addiction means you think you need to use a drug in order to function and feel normal. For example, you may believe that you cannot have fun at a party unless you're drunk or high. Or you may believe that the only way for you to mellow out is to smoke a joint.

If you cannot wait to use drugs, or if you think a lot about using, you are psychologically addicted. You want to be high or drunk as often as you can. You may show up at work or school under the influence of drugs. You may even use drugs while you're at school or work. Drugs are always in the back of your mind. Much of your lifestyle revolves around using drugs or alcohol.

Physical addiction, on the other hand, means that your body needs a drug in order to function and feel normal. If you stop using the drug, your body goes into withdrawal. Without the drug, you feel sick and experience one or

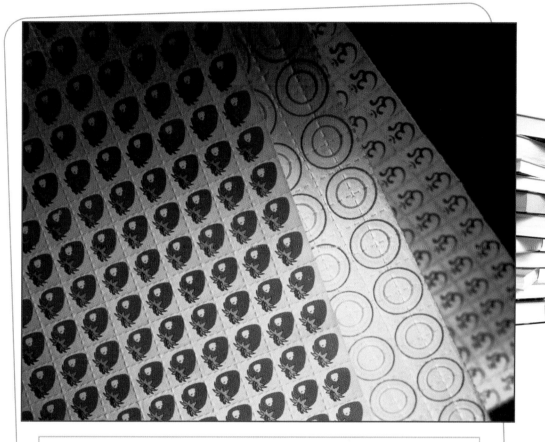

The colorful and cute tabs upon which LSD, or acid, is embedded mask a highly unpredictable drug that can cause poor decision-making, panic, memory loss, brain damage, and psychosis.

more of the following symptoms: nausea, sweating, confusion, depression, insomnia, chills, cramps, and disorientation. Withdrawal from an addiction to depressants is especially dangerous because it can bring on delirium, convulsions, and even death. Those who abuse depressants should quit only under medical supervision.

The Road to Addiction

As you become addicted to a drug, you go through four stages. For some people, it takes several years to go through these stages. Others go through them in a few months. This is because it is easier to become addicted to some drugs than others. Crack and heroin are drugs that you can become addicted to very quickly, even after using them only one or two times.

Stage I: The Gateway

At first, you begin using a drug here and there, mainly for fun. You basically do it because your friends do. You don't have any major problems because of your drug use. There are other things in your life like hobbies, sports, or school. Your drug use doesn't yet interfere with these activities. Some people always stay at this stage. Many teens go through a stage of experimenting with drugs, and then they stop. Others, however, really like what drugs do for them. They end up using more and more. When this happens, they move into the second stage of addiction.

Stage II: Needing More

Now you find yourself needing more of the drug because your tolerance has increased. Small amounts are not good enough. It takes more to make you high or drunk. In order to increase the high, you begin using other drugs. For example, most drug users start with alcohol. Some use marijuana. In this second stage, it's not uncommon to try drugs like LSD, cocaine, or ecstasy. You find yourself thinking about drugs, even when you are not using.

Drugs start to interfere with school or work. You lose interest in school, and you cut class. If you're employed, you may be late for work, miss work altogether, and eventually get fired from your job. You no longer hang out with friends who don't use or drink. You mainly want to be with using or drinking friends. A lot of your money goes toward buying drugs. Things that used to interest you no longer do. You also find yourself feeling more uptight and

Alcohol and drug abuse and criminal behavior often go hand-in-hand. The consequences of substance abuse can be physical injury, emotional pain, and hard jail time and a criminal record.

suspicious. You argue more with people, especially your family. Addiction is starting to set in.

Stage III: Things Fall Apart

By now, it takes large amounts of the substance to get high or drunk. This costs money. You may start selling drugs as a way of getting money. You may do other illegal things to get money. Some drug abusers even turn to prostitution to get drugs.

During this stage, most drug abusers have dropped out of school or lost their jobs. Many leave home or get kicked out. Drug withdrawal occurs. You feel a lot of depression and anger, and you're always uptight. The only way to make these feelings go away is to use more drugs. But when you sober up, the depression and anger always return.

Stage IV: Hitting Rock Bottom

Your drug use is completely out of control. Nothing else is important to you. Your body is so used to drugs that it is hard to get high. Anger, suspicion, and depression are with you every day. Whenever you come down from drugs, the feelings are there.

Physically and mentally, you feel very run-down. Thoughts of suicide come and go. You've had trouble with the law. Maybe you've even been arrested. It's hard to get money for drugs, and you will do anything you have to do to get drugs. When you run out of them, withdrawal is terrible. Some people attempt suicide and end up in the hospital; some people end up in jail. At this point, addiction must be treated with medical and psychological help. If it is not treated properly, addiction can result in death.

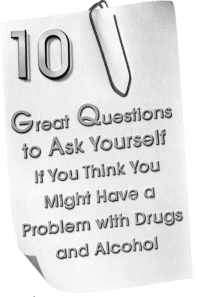

10 Great Questions to Ask Yourself If You Think You Might Have a Problem with Drugs and Alcohol

Here are some questions to ask your-self if you think you might have a problem with drugs and alcohol. If you answer "yes" to more than a couple of these questions, you could be on your way to developing a serious problem. You should seek profes-sional help immediately.

1. Do I use drugs on a regular basis?

2. Are drugs important to me?

3. Do I use drugs when I am alone?

4. Do I use drugs to help me relax or escape my problems?

5. Do I worry if I can't get drugs?

6. Do I mix drugs to get a stronger, more intense high?

7. Do I seek out parties and places where people are using drugs?

8. Have I lied to my family or friends to cover up my drug use?

9. Do I arrange my life around getting high?

10. Do I get angry when people say I have a drug problem?

addiction The dependence on a habit-forming substance so strong that its use causes physical and psychological problems.

asphyxia A loss of consciousness from lack of oxygen and excess of carbon dioxide in the blood.

central nervous system The part of the nervous system consisting of the brain and the spinal cord.

coma A deep unconsciousness from which a person cannot be roused, typically caused by disease or injury.

coordination The normal interaction of body parts, such as eyes and hands, for effective operation.

defense mechanism Mental process of the unconscious that enables a person to cope with painful problems.

denial Unconscious defense mechanism by which one refuses to admit painful thoughts, emotions, or facts.

disorientation The loss of an accurate sense of time, place, or one's own identity.

gene The unit of inheritance of physical and mental traits from one's parents.

hallucination An experience of unreal sights and sounds caused by drug use or illness.

high A state of elation or sense of power caused by the use of a drug.

immune system The system that protects the body from foreign invaders, such as bacteria and viruses.

paranoia Mental disorder in which a person irrationally suspects others of having hostile intentions.

stress Physical or emotional tension created by outside circumstances or events.

Al-Anon/Alateen
1600 Corporate Landing Parkway
Virginia Beach, VA 23454–5617
(757) 563-1600
Web site: http://www.al-anon.alateen.org
This is a twelve-step group for the families and friends
    of alcoholics and drug addicts. Alateen is specifically
    for teenagers.

Alcoholics Anonymous (AA)
P.O. Box 459
New York, NY 10163
(212) 870-3400
Web site: http://www.aa.org
AA is a twelve-step group for alcoholics. It is a proven
    method of helping alcoholics and addicts stay clean.

American Council for Drug Education
50 Jay Street
Brooklyn, NY 11201
(718) 222-6641
Web site: http://www.acde.org
The American Council for Drug Education is a substance
    abuse prevention and education agency that devel-
    ops programs and materials based on the most
    current scientific research on drug use and its impact
    on society.

Canadian Centre on Substance Abuse
75 Albert Street, Suite 500
Ottawa, ON K1P 5E7

Canada
(613) 235-4048
Web site: http://www.ccsa.ca
The Canadian Centre on Substance Abuse provides
    national leadership and evidence-informed analysis
    and advice to mobilize collaborative efforts to reduce
    harms related to drug and alcohol abuse.

Cocaine Anonymous (CA)
21720 South Wilmington Avenue, Suite 304
Long Beach, CA 90810-1641
(310) 559-5833
Web site: http://www.ca.org
CA is a twelve-step program specifically for cocaine addicts.

Kids Help Phone
300-439 University Avenue
Toronto, ON M5G 1Y8
Canada
(416) 586-5437
Web site: http://www.kidshelpphone.ca
Kids Help Phone is Canada's only toll-free, national,
    bilingual phone and Web counseling, referral, and
    information service for children and youth.

Narcotics Anonymous (NA)
P.O. Box 9999
Van Nuys, CA 91409
(818) 773-9999
Web site: http://www.na.org
NA is a twelve-step program for drug addicts of all kinds.

National Clearinghouse for Alcohol and Drug
     Information (NCADI)
1 Choke Cherry Road
Rockville, MD 20857
(877) SAMHSA-7 (726-4727)
Web site: http://www.ncadi.samhsa.gov
NCADI is a resource for information about substance
     abuse prevention and addiction treatment. It has
     information in both English and Spanish.

National Council on Alcoholism and Drug Dependence
     (NCADD)
244 East 58th Street, 4th floor
New York, NY 10022
(212) 269-7797
Web site: http://www.ncadd.org
NCADD provides education, information, help, and hope to
     the public. It advocates prevention, intervention, and
     treatment through a nationwide network of affiliates.

Web Sites

Due to the changing nature of Internet links, Rosen
Publishing has developed an online list of Web sites
related to the subject of this book. This site is updated
regularly. Please use this link to access the list:

http://www.rosenlinks.com/tmh/drug

for further reading

Adams, Colleen. *Rohypnol: Roofies—"The Date Rape Drug"* (Drug Abuse and Society). New York, NY: Rosen Publishing, 2006.

Benson, Michael. *Drug Crime* (Criminal Investigations). New York, NY: Chelsea House, 2008.

Daniels, Peggy. *Drugs* (Issues That Concern You). Farmington Hills, MI: Greenhaven Press, 2011.

DiConsiglio, John. *True Confessions: Real Stories About Drinking and Drugs*. New York, NY: Children's Press, 2008.

Freedman, Jeri. *Steroids* (Drug Abuse Prevention Library). New York, NY: Rosen Publishing, 2009.

Gwinnell, Esther, and Christine A. Adamec. *The Encyclopedia of Drug Abuse*. New York, NY: Facts On File, 2008.

Klosterman, Lorrie. *The Facts About Depressants*. New York, NY: Benchmark Books, 2009.

Lessa, Nicholas R., and Sara Dulaney. *Living with Alcoholism and Drug Abuse* (Teen's Guides). New York, NY: Checkmark Books, 2009.

LeVert, Suzanne. *The Facts About LSD*. New York, NY: Benchmark Books, 2009.

Lookadoo, Justin. *The Dirt on Drugs*. Grand Rapids, MI: Revell, 2008.

Magill, Elizabeth. *Drug Information for Teens: Health Tips About the Physical and Mental Effects of Substance Abuse*. Detroit, MI: Omnigraphics, 2011.

Nelson, David. *Teen Drug Abuse* (Opposing Viewpoints). Farmington Hills, MI: Greenhaven Press, 2010.

Radev, Anna, ed. *I've Got This Friend Who…: Advice for Teens and Their Friends on Alcohol, Drugs, Eating Disorders, Risky Behavior, and More*. Center City, MN: Hazelden Publishing, 2007.

About the Authors

Bruce Edelfield is a writer who lives in Edinburg, New Jersey.

Tracey J. Moosa has written for Rosen Publishing several times on the subjects of drugs, alcohol, and teen emotional health and wellness.

Photo Credits

Cover, p. 1 (top left) © www.istockphoto.com/Diego Cervo; cover, p. 1 (middle left) © www.istockphoto.com/Duncan Walker; cover, p. 1 (bottom left) © www.istockphoto.com/Piotr Marcinski; cover (foreground) © www.istockphoto.com/Adrin Shamsudin; cover, pp. 1, 3 (head and brain) © www.istockphoto.com/Vasily Yakobchuk; p. 3 (laptop) © www.istockphoto.com/Brandon De Suza; pp. 4, 14, 24, 35 (head) © www.istockphoto.com; p. 4 © www.istockphoto.com/ Shelley Perry; p. 6 © www.istockphoto.com/Robert Kohlhuber; pp. 7, 14,17 Shutterstock; p. 11 AFP/AFP via Getty Images; p. 18 © www. istockphoto.com/Paul Hill; p. 19 DEA; p. 21 Bloomberg/Bloomberg via Getty Images; p. 24 © www.istockphoto.com/ericsphotography; p. 25 istockphoto/Thinkstock; p. 26 Toby Canham/Getty Images Entertainment/Getty Images; p. 29 © www.istockphoto.com/Eric Honeycutt; p. 31 3D4Medical/Photo Researchers; p. 32 © www. istockphoto.com/John Rodriguez; p. 35 © www.istockphoto.com/ Ivar Teunissen; p. 37 Tek Image/Photo Researchers; p. 39 Chris Ryan/OJO Images/Getty Images; interior graphics (books) © www.istockphoto.com/Michal Koziarski.

Photo Researcher: Marty Levick